Humanitarian Organizations

The Peace Corps

Terry Hastings

CHELSEA HOUSE
PUBLISHERS

A Haights Cross Communications ✈ Company ®

Philadelphia

For my parents Bess and Eric Hastings.

This edition first published in 2006 in the United States of America by Chelsea House Publishers, a subsidiary of Haights Cross Communications.

A Haights Cross Communications ✦ Company ®

Chelsea House Publishers
2080 Cabot Boulevard West, Suite 201
Langhorne, PA 19047-1813

The Chelsea House world wide web address is www.chelseahouse.com

First published in 2005 by
MACMILLAN EDUCATION AUSTRALIA PTY LTD
627 Chapel Street, South Yarra 3141

Visit our website at www.macmillan.com.au

Associated companies and representatives throughout the world.

Copyright © Terry Hastings 2005

Library of Congress Cataloging-in-Publication Data applied for.
ISBN 0 7910 8812 X

Edited by Anna Fern
Text and cover design by Raul Diche
Page layout by Raul Diche
Photo research by Legend Images
Maps by Pat Kermode

Printed in China

Acknowledgments
The author and publisher are grateful to the Peace Corps for its assistance and advice in the preparation of this book.

The author and the publisher are also grateful to the Peace Corps for supplying the photographs for this book, and to Amnesty International Australia, Australian Red Cross, Greenpeace, Doctors Without Borders/ Médicins Sans Frontières (MSF), the Peace Corps and Save the Children for their permission to reproduce the logos on page 4.

Every care has been taken to trace and acknowledge copyright. Where the attempt has been unsuccessful, the publisher welcomes information that would redress the situation.

Please note
At the time of printing, the Internet addresses appearing in this book were correct. Owing to the dynamic nature of the Internet, however, we cannot guarantee that all these addresses will remain correct.

Contents

Glossary words

When a word is printed in **bold**, its meaning is included on that page. You can also look up its meaning in the Glossary on page 31.

What is a Humanitarian Organization?

Humanitarian organizations work to help solve problems in countries around the world, wherever there is a need for their help. They are sometimes called aid agencies, non-profit, or non-governmental organizations (NGOs).

Some organizations, such as Greenpeace, work to protect the environment. Others, such as Amnesty International and the International Red Cross, work to protect people's **human rights** or provide for their basic needs in times of conflict and disaster. Doctors Without Borders sends **volunteers** anywhere in the world to give medical help to people affected by disasters. Groups such as the Peace Corps and Save the Children help communities who need education and medical support. The Peace Corps also supports agricultural projects, assists disadvantaged youth, and helps people to set up small businesses.

Some humanitarian organizations are given money by governments to help run their programs. They also work hard to collect enough money from the public to keep going. Some of their workers are volunteers and are not paid, while others work for a small wage or are given a **living allowance**.

The *Humanitarian Organizations* series focuses on six well-known organizations and explains how they help those in need around the world.

Glossary words

human rights
a set of rights, such as the right to a fair trial, laid down by the United Nations

volunteers
people who donate their time to a cause

living allowance
a small amount of money for everyday needs

The Peace Corps

The Red Cross

Greenpeace

Save the Children

Amnesty International

Doctors Without Borders

About the Peace Corps

The Peace Corps is an American organization that helps **developing countries**. It assists communities at a practical level, and promotes the cause of world peace and friendship through international understanding and **cross-cultural exchange**. President John F. Kennedy established the Peace Corps in 1961, and since 1981, it has been an **independent agency** of the United States government.

The work of the Peace Corps was summed up in President Kennedy's first speech after he became President. He said, "To those people in the huts and villages of half the globe struggling to break the bonds of mass misery, we pledge our best efforts to help them help themselves."

Helping Communities

The Peace Corps recruits and trains Volunteers from the United States, who then go to developing countries to live and work for a period of two years. These men and women serve as teachers in elementary and secondary schools, work to help protect the environment, or teach farmers how to grow food more efficiently. Other Peace Corps Volunteers (PCVs) assist people to set up small businesses or help communities prevent the spread of diseases such as malaria and **HIV/AIDS**.

More than 178,000 Volunteers have worked in 138 countries throughout the world since the Peace Corps began.

This is the logo for the Peace Corps.

History of the Peace Corps

In October 1960, presidential candidate Senator John F. Kennedy made a late-night visit to the University of Michigan. He wanted to rest from a tiring election campaign, but 10,000 students were eagerly waiting to hear him speak. He could not disappoint them.

Challenging the Youth of America

In his speech, Senator Kennedy outlined an idea for a Peace Corps. He challenged the young men and women of America to serve their country and the cause of peace by living and working in the developing world.

Later that year, Kennedy was elected President of the United States. He made the setting up of the Peace Corps one of his first priorities.

On October 14, 1960, at 2:00 A.M., John F. Kennedy spoke to students at the University of Michigan about his idea for a Peace Corps.

Choosing the Best

The Peace Corps began officially on March 1, 1961, when President Kennedy signed a document to set it up. He appointed Sargent Shriver as the first Peace Corps Director. Recruitment of Peace Corps Volunteers (PCVs) soon began. The PCVs would become representatives of the United States in overseas countries, so it was important to choose only the best applicants. All potential PCVs had to pass a strict written test to find out if they had the right skills, education, and attitude.

Did you know?

The close association between President Kennedy and the Peace Corps led to Volunteers becoming known as "Kennedy's Kids."

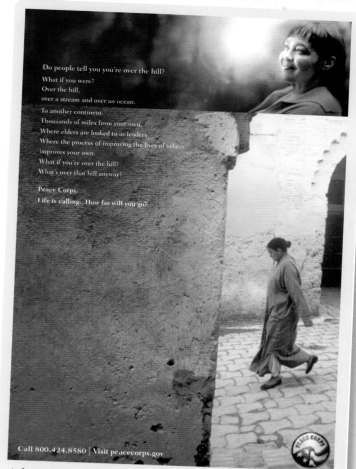

Do people tell you you're over the hill?
What if you were?
Over the hill,
over a stream and over an ocean.
To another continent.
Thousands of miles from your own.
Where elders are looked to as leaders.
Where the process of improving the lives of others improves your own.
What if you're over the hill?
What's over that hill anyway?

Peace Corps.
Life is calling. How far will you go?

Call 800.424.8580 | Visit peacecorps.gov

Advertising campaigns like this are very successful in attracting Volunteers to the Peace Corps.

Growth of the Peace Corps

Interest in the Peace Corps began slowly, but more applicants were attracted through better advertising and intense recruiting campaigns on university campuses. The first PCVs went to Ghana and Tanzania, in Africa. By 1966, the number of Volunteers in the field had grown to an all-time high of 15,000.

The Peace Corps has now been operating for more than 40 years, and continues to expand. In 1990, its first Volunteers began work in Hungary and Poland. More recently, the first Peace Corps Volunteers arrived in parts of the former Soviet Union, China, and South Africa. They included highly qualified specialists such as **agronomists**, and **engineers**, and those with advanced degrees.

Looking Ahead

Thousands of Peace Corps Volunteers are still assisting individuals, communities, and nations around the world. Like the PCVs before them, they are learning the languages and customs of their host countries. In the process, they make international friendships that help them understand the people of different countries. Their work also helps people in those countries to understand Americans and to become familiar with **democratic values**. Most importantly, after the Peace Corps Volunteers return to the United States, they work to educate Americans about the people and cultures of different countries. Returned Volunteers frequently speak in schools, community centers, and churches.

Did you know?

The average Peace Corps Volunteer is 28 years old, but six percent of PCVs are older than 50, and the oldest is 82.

The Founders of the Peace Corps

The idea for a Peace Corps had been discussed since the 1950s. The term "Peace Corps," however, was used for the first time in 1960 when Senator Hubert Humphrey spoke in the United States Congress, saying that he wanted "young men to assist the peoples of the underdeveloped areas of the world to combat poverty, disease, **illiteracy**, and hunger."

From Dream to Reality

United States President John F. Kennedy was the founder of the Peace Corps. His decision to establish the organization was based on the belief that desperation and misery lead to revolution and war. The work of Peace Corps Volunteers would help to overcome these problems and contribute to world peace. The Volunteers' practical skills would fight poverty, while their international friendships would help Americans and people in other countries to learn about one another.

Active Leadership

Sargent Shriver, the first Director, was another very important figure. His encouragement and commitment were vital to the success of the Peace Corps. He shared President Kennedy's vision, and worked actively to make the Peace Corps an effective humanitarian organization.

Sargent Shriver (left) was given the job of first Director of the Peace Corps by President Kennedy (right).

Since that time, many notable individuals have served as Director of the Peace Corps. They have improved the agency by doing things like introducing new programs, expanding projects to Eastern Europe, and recruiting Volunteers from America's different ethnic groups.

Glossary word

illiteracy
inability to read and write

Did you know?

Poverty is associated with rapid population growth, bad health conditions, and inequality between men and women.

Early Work

In 1961, the first Peace Corps Volunteers left to work on assignments in the African nations of Ghana and Tanzania. The 51 Volunteers who landed in Ghana certainly made a big impression. As a sign of friendship, they sang the Ghanaian national anthem in the local language.

Only two years later, the number of Volunteers had grown to 7,300. They served in 44 countries, from Afghanistan to Uruguay. More than half worked in education, a quarter in **community development**, and the rest in agriculture, health care, and public works. By June 1966, there were more than 15,000 Volunteers working overseas. It was an all-time record for the Peace Corps.

The 1970s brought changes and challenges to the Peace Corps. For a time, it was combined with other volunteer groups into a single new agency, but, by 1979, it again became a separate organization. The Volunteers were more qualified and older than before, and included doctors, engineers, and **horticulturists**. They passed on their skills to people in the host countries who, in turn, shared them with their fellow citizens.

At the close of the decade, more than 6,000 Volunteers were at work, and two returned Volunteers had been elected to the United States Senate.

Did you know?

President Kennedy honored the first Peace Corps Volunteers in a special ceremony at the White House rose garden.

Glossary words

community development the building of stronger communities (e.g., through help for women's groups or support for teenagers)

horticulturists experts in growing flowers, fruit, and vegetables

President Kennedy meets some of the first Peace Corps Volunteers.

Core Values of the Peace Corps

Core values are the things that a person, group, or organization really believes in. The values are used to work out rules of behavior. The Peace Corps promotes world peace and friendship and expresses its core values in the form of the following mission statement:

- to help the people of interested countries in meeting their need for trained men and women
- to help promote a better understanding of Americans in countries where Volunteers serve
- to help promote a better understanding of people of other nations, by Americans.

Peace Corps Volunteers face the challenging task of putting these beliefs into practice. They do this in the following ways:

Building Communities

Peace Corps Volunteers work with community leaders in interested countries. Together, they help to achieve change that will last beyond the time a Volunteer is helping with the effort.

Setting Examples

Peace Corps Volunteers must be fair and honest in their personal lives. They develop friendships with the people they serve and help them to understand Americans.

Respecting Others

Peace Corps Volunteers treasure the common bonds that all humans share. They treat people as individuals and respect the cultures and traditions of their host countries.

A Peace Corps Volunteer at work, teaching in Kazakhstan.

Did you know?

Before beginning their assignments, Peace Corps Volunteers receive three months of language instruction, technical skills training, health education, and cross-cultural orientation.

How the Peace Corps Works

The Peace Corps headquarters is in Washington, D.C. There, the Director and senior staff manage the operations of the Peace Corps throughout the world.

The Director is the chief of the organization and is appointed by the President of the United States. Other managers look after separate areas such as training, finance, recruitment, and the health and safety of Volunteers while they are in service.

The Volunteers

Volunteers are the heart and soul of the Peace Corps. As more countries ask for Volunteers, the Peace Corps must recruit new people. It runs recruiting campaigns on university and college campuses throughout the United States, and advertises for Volunteers at conferences, and with donated television, radio, and print ads. Age, race, and ethnic background are no barriers to Peace Corps service, but all Volunteers must be United States citizens, older than 18, and in reasonable health.

Returned Volunteers

Returned Peace Corps Volunteers (RPCVs) make a great contribution to the Peace Corps. They publish newsletters to keep members up-to-date with current happenings. Many local groups of RPCVs meet regularly to support recruitment. They also visit schools, community centers, and churches to talk to students about their experiences and help them understand the cultures and countries in which they served.

Did you know?

Directors of the Peace Corps have included men and women of Asian, Jewish, and Hispanic heritage.

Gaddi H. Vasquez is the 16th Director of the Peace Corps. President George W. Bush appointed him to the position.

Where in the World is the Peace Corps?

The Peace Corps has worked in many regions around the world. This map shows the regions where Volunteers have served from 1961 to 2004. The key lists the countries from those regions.

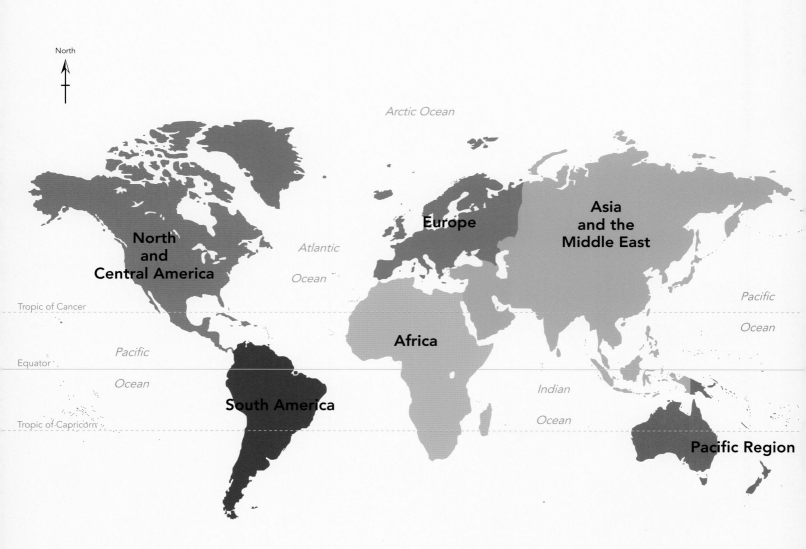

Timeline

Key to countries

PACIFIC REGION
Federated States of Micronesia, Fiji, Kiribati, Marshall Islands, New Guinea, Palau, Samoa, Solomon Islands, Tonga, Tuvalu, Vanuatu

AFRICA
Benin, Botswana, Burkina Faso, Burundi, Cabinda (Angola), Cameroon, Cape Verde, Central African Republic, Chad, Côte d'Ivoire, Democratic Republic of the Congo, Eritrea, Equatorial Guinea, Ethiopia, Gabon, Gambia, Ghana, Guinea, Guinea-Bissau, Kenya, Lesotho, Liberia, Libya, Madagascar, Malawi, Mali, Mauritania, Mauritius, Morocco, Mozambique, Namibia, Niger, Nigeria, Republic of Congo, Rwanda, São Tomé and Principe, Senegal, Seychelles, Sierra Leone, Somalia, South Africa, Sudan, Swaziland, Tanzania, Togo, Tunisia, Uganda, Zambia, Zimbabwe

ASIA AND THE MIDDLE EAST
Afghanistan, Armenia, Azerbaijan, Bahrain, Bangladesh, China, Cyprus, East Timor, India, Iran, Jordan, Kazakhstan, Kyrgyz Republic, Malaysia, Mongolia, Nepal, Oman, Pakistan, Philippines, Singapore, South Korea, Thailand, Turkmenistan, Uzbekistan, Yemen

NORTH AND CENTRAL AMERICA
Belize, Costa Rica, Dominican Republic, El Salvador, Guatemala, Haiti, Honduras, Jamaica, Mexico, Nicaragua, Panama

SOUTH AMERICA
Argentina, Bolivia, Brazil, Chile, Colombia, Ecuador, Guyana, Paraguay, Peru, Suriname, Uruguay, Venezuela

EUROPE
Albania, Bulgaria, Czech Republic, Estonia, Georgia, Hungary, Lithuania, Macedonia, Malta, Moldova, Romania, Russia, Slovakia, Turkey, Ukraine

---

The Peace Corps has been working to help people since it began in 1961.

1960	Senator John F. Kennedy addresses students at the University of Michigan and challenges them to serve their country in a proposed Peace Corps.
1961	Peace Corps is officially founded by President Kennedy. The first Volunteers leave for Ghana and Tanzania, in Africa.
1963	7,300 Peace Corps Volunteers serve in 44 countries.
1964	Peace Corps Partnerships Project allows Americans at home to support and contribute to Volunteer projects overseas.
1966	The number of serving Peace Corps Volunteers reaches 15,000.
1971	During the Nixon administration, the Peace Corps loses its separate identity when, with other volunteer organizations, it is absorbed into ACTION.
1979	President Jimmy Carter gives the Peace Corps its own independent management and identity.
1981	The Peace Corps celebrates its 20th anniversary.
1985	The Peace Corps Fellow Program at Teachers College, Columbia University, is set up to train returned Peace Corps Volunteers as teachers for New York public schools.
1989	The Coverdell World Wise Schools program enables American students to learn about the work of the Peace Corps and to correspond with serving Peace Corps Volunteers.
1990s	Peace Corps Volunteers serve for the first time in countries such as China, Estonia, Hungary, Latvia, Lithuania, Poland, and South Africa.
1995	Crisis Corps is established to allow Peace Corps Volunteers and returned Peace Corps Volunteers to help in times of natural disaster and crisis.
1998	The Peace Corps moves to its own headquarters in Washington, D.C.
2004	7,733 Volunteers and trainees are either serving or preparing to help communities in other parts of the world. President George W. Bush promotes the work of the Peace Corps in order to attract more Volunteers for service in the 21st century.

Inadequate Education

The Peace Corps is concerned that about 140 million children in the world do not have a basic education. Two-thirds of these children are girls. Their lack of education often limits future opportunities, causing poverty and poor health throughout their lives.

Research shows there is a strong link between girls' education and the general well-being of society. This is because education enables girls to learn about health issues and to acquire valuable skills that make them more successful as mothers. Education also increases their opportunities to earn money, which benefits the health and financial situation of their families.

Social expectations can prevent girls from gaining further education. In the West African country of Niger, parents often expect their daughters to marry at age 14 or 15, and they see no use in girls continuing at school after marriage. Girls in many countries also have important responsibilities at home, such as fetching water and firewood or caring for younger children while their parents are at work. They cannot go to school as well. Some girls live in rural areas where the nearest school is far away. Others are pressured to find jobs and help support their families. All these circumstances put girls at a disadvantage.

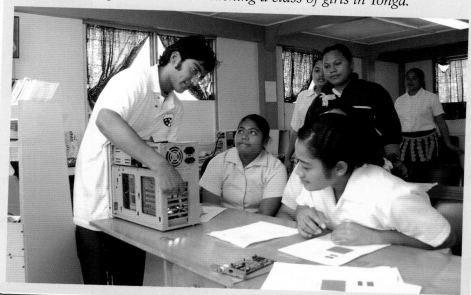

This Peace Corps Volunteer is teaching a class of girls in Tonga.

To help girls to continue at school, Peace Corps Volunteers:

- encourage girls to answer questions, assume responsibilities, and participate actively in classroom activities
- set up single-sex classes and clubs, special camps, and scholarships which help girls to develop self-esteem and to value high achievement at school
- act as role models for female students and offer them counseling and guidance
- establish childcare centers near schools, where girls can leave their own children or younger brothers and sisters while they are in class.

Peace Corps Volunteers also try to build support for girls by getting the cooperation of their parents, government officials, and local religious and community leaders.

Education will open up many opportunities for these girls in Botswana.

Classic action

In the West African country of Guinea, Peace Corps Volunteers started a women's magazine called *Aïcha*. Guinean girls contribute most of the articles, gaining confidence in their reading and writing skills. The magazine's topics have included women's education, women's health issues, and early marriage. Volunteers help to change attitudes by discussing *Aïcha* with their female students and other women who can read and write.

HIV/AIDS Educator

Adeyemi Oshodi (front row) with the eight young Swazi writers she helped to train.

It is a long way from Columbus, Ohio, to Swaziland, in southern Africa. Nevertheless, Adeyemi Oshodi made that journey. She now helps to reduce the spread of HIV/AIDS by serving as a youth educator in the rural Swazi community of Mpolonjeni.

Adeyemi originally trained as a journalist. As a Peace Corps Volunteer, she has used her abilities to set up the Mpolonjeni Journalism Club with eight Swazi youth members. They began by working hard for four months to improve their journalism skills and to gain more knowledge of HIV/AIDS.

The members now serve the community as reporters, writers, and photographers. They produce a monthly HIV/AIDS and youth issues newsletter called *Umbono Wetfu* or *Our Opinion*. Its interesting and original articles can include "a day in the life" of a local rural health motivator, personal statements from individuals recently tested for HIV, or poems and fiction work on youth issues.

Once a month, the members of *Umbono Wetfu* also work on a "community advancement" project. These projects assist people in the community who have asked for help. After writing a story about the individual, the group does something to help the family, from cleaning their homestead to conducting fundraising activities.

Another thing the club does is to donate food to a *gogo*, or grandmother, in the community who is struggling to raise her 10 orphaned grandchildren, after her own children died of AIDS.

Did you know?

Swaziland has the highest rate of HIV infection in the world. More than one-third of its people have the disease and thousands of parents have died, leaving their children as orphans.

At the formal launching of the club and newsletter, the club members showed how much they had learned about communication. "When the *Umbono Wetfu* youth stood in front of the crowd last week, discussing their work and personal growth since joining the team, I looked on with such satisfaction," Adeyemi says.

The launching truly developed into a great day for the community. There were enough donated chickens, other food, and money to feed more than 300 people. Members of Parliament and HIV/AIDS organizations gave speeches. Local youth groups performed songs and dances about youth issues and played HIV/AIDS-awareness games with the audience, giving out prizes and T-shirts.

Adeyemi would like her project to continue long after her service ends. She speaks for everyone in the club when she says "We hope the youth and the community take control of this project, as they did during the launching."

Did you know?

The Peace Corps was first invited to work in Swaziland in 1969, a few months after the country gained independence from Great Britain.

Another Peace Corps Volunteer, Brigid O'Brien, and her host mother in Swaziland.

What Can You Do?

There are many ways you can help the Peace Corps in its work.

During Peace Corps Week, students in Washington, D.C. meet a returned Peace Corps Volunteer.

Coverdell World Wise Schools

Some groups of young people connect with Peace Corps Volunteers by joining the CyberVolunteer program through Coverdell World Wise Schools. After signing up online at **www.peacecorps.gov/wws**, their classes receive monthly letters from serving Volunteers. The program helps to raise awareness and spread the message of international friendship.

Peace Corps Partnerships

Young people can also sponsor a Peace Corps Volunteer, or donate money to a particular community project. They can exchange letters and photos with Volunteers.

www.peacecorps.gov/index.cfm?shell=resources.donors

Peace Corps Week

Young people can promote world peace and friendship by celebrating Peace Corps Week. This event is held every year in the first week of March. Many students decorate their classrooms, contact local newspapers and TV stations or invite returned Peace Corps Volunteers to talk about their experiences. More information can be found on the Internet at **www.peacecorps.com/pcweek**.

Community Projects

Getting involved in your own community can help the Peace Corps to make a better world. Some ideas are:
- tutoring non-English-speaking students
- organizing a Read-a-Thon in your school
- writing letters to newspapers to encourage an environmental clean-up.

The "Kids World" Web site at **www.peacecorps.gov/kids/** has lots of information on the work of the Peace Corps around the world, and shows what you can do to make a difference.

Glossary

agronomists	experts in land management and crop production
community development	the building of stronger communities (e.g., through help for women's groups or support for teenagers)
cross-cultural exchange	the sharing of customs, opinions, and traditions between people of different cultures
democratic values	standards that guide the behavior of governments and individuals in democratic societies, including the right to participate in the political process
developing countries	countries that are not yet able to provide a good standard of living for their citizens in such areas as health, education, and housing
engineers	experts who design and manage the construction of public works, such as railways, bridges, drains, and roads
evacuated	taken from a dangerous place to somewhere safer
free market	a system where businesses compete freely without government controls
HIV/AIDS	a virus that stops the body from fighting against infections
horticulturists	experts in growing flowers, fruit, and vegetables
human rights	a set of rights, such as the right to a fair trial, laid down by the United Nations
illiteracy	inability to read and write
independent agency	an office funded by the United States government, but having decision-making powers of its own
living allowance	a small amount of money for everyday needs
outreach	going out to people in the community to provide them with information or services
sanitation	proper removal of garbage and sewage
value-added products	products that have been manufactured or processed to increase their value
volunteers	people who donate their time to a cause
youth development officers	people who advise young people and assist them to develop good values and practical work skills

Index